SPOTLIGHT ON NATIVE AMERICANS

HOPI

Ivy Kuszewski

press.

New York

Published in 2016 by The Rosen Publishing Group, Inc.
29 East 21st Street, New York, NY 10010

First Edition

Editor: Karolena Bielecki
Book Design: Kris Everson
Reviewed by: Robert J. Conley, Former Sequoyah Distinguished Professor at Western Carolina University and Director of Native American Studies at Morningside College and Montana State University
Supplemental material reviewed by: Donald A. Grinde, Jr., Professor of Transnational/American Studies at the State University of New York at Buffalo.

Photo Credits: Cover Universal Images Group/SuperStock; pp. 4–5 Rich Reid; pp. 7, 15, 20, 23 Peter Newark's American Pictures; pp. 9, 10, 13, 29 Corbis; pp. 16–17 Witold Skrypczak; p. 19 Mary Evans/Picture Library Ltd; p. 21 John Cancalosi; p. 24 Native Stock; p. 25 FBethanis; p. 27 Time & Life Pictures.

Library of Congress Cataloging-in-Publication Data

Kuszewski, Ivy.
  Hopi / Ivy Kuszewski.
      pages cm. — (Spotlight on Native Americans)
  Includes bibliographical references and index.
  ISBN 978-1-4994-1661-9 (pbk.)
  ISBN 978-1-4994-1660-2 (6 pack)
  ISBN 978-1-4994-1663-3 (library binding)
  1. Hopi Indians—History—Juvenile literature. 2. Hopi Indians—Social life and customs—Juvenile literature. I. Title.
  E99.H7K89 2015
  979.1004'97458—dc23
                                          2015007810

Manufactured in the United States of America

CPSIA Compliance Information: Batch #WS15PK: For Further Information contact Rosen Publishing, New York, New York at 1-800-237-9932

CONTENTS

THE PEACEFUL PEOPLE 4

A LONG HISTORY 6

CONTACT WITH AMERICANS 8

HOPI LIFE IN THE EARLY TWENTIETH CENTURY . . .10

HOPI LIFE IN THE LATER TWENTIETH CENTURY . . .12

TRADITIONAL HOPI LIFESTYLE 14

HOPI SOCIAL STRUCTURE 16

FAMILY LIFE 18

CEREMONIES 20

CONTEMPORARY HOPIS 22

HOPI ARTS 24

THE HOPI ECONOMY 26

HOPI ISSUES TODAY 28

GLOSSARY 30

FOR MORE INFORMATION 31

INDEX 32

THE PEACEFUL PEOPLE

CHAPTER 1

The word *Hopi* has been defined as "peaceful people," "righteous," or "virtuous." The westernmost group of **Pueblo Indians**, the Hopis live on a 1.6 million-acre (648,000 ha) **reservation** in northeastern Arizona. It is a limited portion of their traditional lands and completely surrounded by the Navajo Reservation. According to the U.S. Census Bureau, the population of the Hopi reservation is over 12,000. People live in 14 villages on top of three **mesas**: First Mesa, Second Mesa, and Third Mesa. The Hopis have lived in this area for at least 1,000 years.

According to Hopi traditional beliefs, Tawa, the Sun Spirit, created all people. Gogyeng Sowuhti, known as the Spider Grandmother, and the boy warrior gods, named Pokanghoya and Polongahoya, led the people with good hearts into the Fourth World (this world). Evil people were left behind in the Third World, found beneath this one. The good people climbed a reed through a hole in the sky. The Fourth World was empty except for Masauwu, the god of fire and death, who welcomed them.

Yawpa, the mockingbird, divided the people into different tribes. These tribes traveled to find their homes. The Hopis settled in an area that is now called Black Mesa, Arizona.

Called "the oldest people" by other tribes, Hopis have lived for centuries in the dry, open countryside called the Black Mesa in Arizona.

5

A LONG HISTORY
CHAPTER 2

For 850 years, Hopis have lived in Oraibi, Arizona, the oldest surviving settlement in the United States. The Hopis successfully farmed corn in the desert landscape. They mined coal for baking pottery, cooking, and heating. The people built **kivas**, underground rooms, for complex ceremonies. They also defended themselves against raids by Navajos and other Native American tribes.

In 1540, Hopis in Oraibi's neighboring town of Awatovi met the Spanish explorer Pedro de Tovar. Sent to find gold, de Tovar discovered the Hopis had none and left.

In 1629, priests arrived in Awatovi and built a Christian **mission**. They had little effect on Hopi traditional beliefs. However, the people in the mission introduced new livestock, crops, and metal tools to the Hopis.

In 1680, the Hopis joined with other Pueblo peoples in the Pueblo **Revolt** against the Spanish. Twelve years later, the Spanish once again conquered the Pueblo peoples. Disagreement spread among the Hopis. Some

Explorer Francisco Vásquez de Coronado and his soldiers crossed the southwestern United States in search of the fabled Seven Cities of Gold in 1540 at the request of the king of Spain, who had heard rumors of great riches north of Mexico.

wanted to live like the Christians, and others wanted to continue their traditional lifestyle. In 1700, the traditional Hopis killed the Christian men, destroying Awatovi. From 1823 to 1845, the Mexican governors in Santa Fe, New Mexico, failed to prevent raids on Hopi **pueblos**.

CONTACT WITH AMERICANS

CHAPTER 3

In 1846, the United States and Mexico began a war over which country held present-day Texas. When the United States won the war in 1848, it gained a vast amount of territory, including Texas, California, Nevada, Utah, and most of Arizona as well as parts of other present-day U.S. states. Hopi lands thus became a part of the United States.

In 1849, the U.S. government named John Calhoun to act as Indian agent and govern the southwestern tribes. Then, in 1874, the Keams Canyon government agency was built, as were three Christian missions. Without consulting the Hopis, President Chester Arthur established a reservation, where all members of the tribe were supposed to live, in 1882. However, the new Hopi reservation covered only one-tenth of their traditional lands.

The creation of a **boarding school** at Keams Canyon in 1887 deeply affected traditional Hopi society. Hopi children were forced to attend the school, where they learned the English language and American customs. Congress passed the Dawes Severalty Act the same

Hopi men traveled to Santa Fe, New Mexico, to ask John Calhoun, Indian agent and later governor of the territory, for help in defending themselves against Navajo raids.

year, requiring tribes to divide their reservation and give each family one piece of land. The traditional Hopis fought this law, and many were sent to prison. In the end, the Hopis kept their reservation whole.

HOPI LIFE IN THE EARLY TWENTIETH CENTURY

CHAPTER 4

During the early 1900s, disagreements among the Hopis created the worst problems the tribe had yet faced. Hopis divided into two different sides: the U.S. government reports named them the "Friendlies" and the "Hostiles." The Friendlies were

The traditional Pueblo Indian architecture of Old Oraibi featured an **adobe** and stone "apartment building." Hopis could climb to the top floor by stone stairs or by ladder.

in favor of learning English and cooperating with the government. Today, they are called "Progressives." Called the "Traditionalists" today, the Hostiles did not want any changes to the Hopi lifestyle.

In 1906, Youkeoma, leader of the Hostiles, drew a line in the sand and said that he and his people would leave Oraibi if the Friendlies' leader, Tewaquaptewa, could push him across the line. After a long pushing contest, he was pushed over the line, and the Hostiles left Oraibi to begin a new traditional village called Hotevilla. Oraibi continued to lose people until it became a dying village of only 100 people instead of a lively center of 600.

The 1934 Indian Reorganization Act provided a way for Native American nations to establish their own tribal government; each tribe voted whether to accept the act. Though most Hopis refused to vote in the tribal election, the Hopi Tribal Council was formed in 1936. The council functioned only occasionally until the 1950s.

HOPI LIFE IN THE LATE TWENTIETH CENTURY

CHAPTER 5

With World War II (1939–1945) came an increase in the number of Hopis moving off the reservation. Some fought in the war, while some **conscientious objectors** left the reservation to provide other services to the country, such as nursing or working in factories to aid the war effort.

The tribal council was revived in the 1950s to deal with outsiders, such as U.S. government officials and other non-Hopis, but the 12 Hopi villages each governed themselves. All but one of the villages favored the traditional Hopi form of government, which was led by a *kikmongwi*, or village chief.

In 1960, the new tribal council **sued** the Navajo tribe. The Hopis claimed that Navajo settlers **trespassed** on the Hopi Reservation as established in 1882. Finally, in 1974, the U.S. government passed the Navajo-Hopi Land Settlement Act. According to the law, Hopis who lived on Navajo land were supposed to move to the Hopi land, and the Navajos on Hopi

During World War II, Private Floyd Dann, a Hopi, spoke to other tribal members in the U.S. Army using a code based on the Hopi language. The enemy side could not figure out the code, making this a useful way of passing information during wartime.

land were to move to Navajo land. While most of the Hopis left Navajo land, many Navajo families on Hopi land did not, having lived there for generations. Both sides are unhappy with the current situation, and **negotiations** continue to this day.

TRADITIONAL HOPI LIFESTYLE

CHAPTER 6

The Hopis were farmers, growing many varieties of corn, beans, squash, and cotton. After they met the Spanish, they traded these crops for animals such as horses and sheep, as well as for peaches and apricots. They also traded with the people from Mexico for chili peppers.

Each Hopi village took care of its own people. There was no **private property**; different **clans** owned the fields along the waterways below the villages. While the fields belonged to the women in each clan, their husbands, brothers, and sons planted and cared for the crops.

Many wild plants growing nearby proved useful for making shampoo, hairbrushes, brooms, baskets, and trays. The Hopis hunted rabbits and traded for other goods that they needed.

Hopi men contributed their work to the household where they lived—their mother's, wife's, or sister's household. They also wove material, usually for ceremonial clothing of white cotton and wool, while the women made pottery.

Hopi men hunted rabbits with a curved stick that was thrown with deadly accuracy at the racing cottontails.

The women ground the corn and cooked a variety of meals with it. One of the most common foods was called *piki*, a paper-thin bread made of blue corn that was cooked on a special hot piki stone found in every Hopi household.

HOPI SOCIAL STRUCTURE

CHAPTER 7

All Hopi people belonged to a clan, a group of relatives of a person's mother. Hopi households contained just one family, but often included the mother's other relatives. Originally, 75 clans existed, but today there are 34 Hopi clans, including the Cloud, Spider, Snake, Bear, Butterfly, and Eagle clans. Each clan has its own kachina (a form of spirit being) and special responsibilities in the village and during ceremonies.

Hopis also belonged to societies made up of members of various clans. There were fewer societies than clans.

Members of the societies were leaders for the important ceremonies. Important ceremonies such as *Soyal* (the winter **solstice** ceremony) had their own societies to govern them, and all adult men belonged to the Kachina Society as well as at least one other society.

Each Hopi village was independent and governed itself. Typically, the village chief, or *kikmongwi*, chose and trained the next leader, but the villagers had to approve the choice. Usually the head of the Bear Clan, the *kikmongwi* led the village, solved problems, and worked with outsiders. The second-in-command, the village crier, called out the news and announcements as he walked through the village each morning.

The left-hand image in these rock carvings at Betatakin, a cliff village in Arizona, represents the Hopi Fire clan.

FAMILY LIFE

CHAPTER 8

Hopi families hid their babies from the sun for 19 days after birth. On the 20th day, the baby's grandmother named it in a family ceremony. The baby was then blessed with cornmeal and taken outside to meet the sun at dawn.

Children learned how to do things by helping their parents. They might begin by gathering firewood or helping adults pick fruits and plants. Soon the boys learned how to hunt rabbits, grow corn, and weave cloth. The girls learned how to grind corn and make piki bread, baskets, and pottery. Children spent time playing games. Adults told stories to teach children about Hopi history, religion, **culture**, and the proper way to behave.

Both boys and girls were **initiated** into a society at age seven, where they were given another name. Then boys could enter the kivas. When girls were ready to marry, they had a corn-grinding ceremony and put their hair up into a special "squash-blossom" style over their ears, which they wore until they were married. **Adolescent** boys had a second initiation into one of

This painting shows a Hopi girl's hair being arranged "squash-blossom," a style worn until marriage. Today, young women wear this time-consuming style only on special occasions.

four societies—singer, horn, agave, or *wuwuchim* (which means New Fire Ceremony)—between ages 16 and 20 to begin participating fully in ceremonial life.

CEREMONIES
CHAPTER 9

Most ceremonies were held to honor and communicate with the spirits, asking for life, rain, and good crops. In the Hopi desert country, everything depended upon rain, and this was reflected in their ceremonial life. Organized in the villages, the important ceremonies lasted for eight or more days. The first part of most ceremonies included secret **rituals** performed in the kivas. Involving the public, the

This picture, made in 1910, shows dancers in the plaza during a Hopi harvest ceremony, which was probably one of the women's ceremonies that took place in September.

This young Hopi girl is dressed in traditional makeup and clothing for a social dance on the Hopi reservation.

second part of the ceremony happened in a central plaza and was more festive.

Some ceremonies were women's ceremonies, and some were social events. The Hopi societies put on the ceremonies, but certain things could only be done by specific clan members; for example, a man of the Sand clan had to bring sand to make the altar in one ceremony.

Ceremonies started when the village crier called everyone to gather. Many times, offerings of feathered prayer sticks, or *pahos*, were placed on altars and in other sacred places. Many of these ceremonies continue today.

CONTEMPORARY HOPIS

CHAPTER 10

Hopi children are raised in a traditional manner in their homes, but they attend the same kinds of schools non-Hopi children attend. They may still speak Hopi at home and participate in the Hopi societies when they are old enough. All children are involved with their parents in Hopi ceremonies and must learn the differences between over 200 different kachinas.

Despite the traditional lifestyle on the reservation, many young people leave the reservation to find work elsewhere, including jobs provided by the U.S. Army. Jobs on the reservation include working at the Hopi Cultural Center on the Second Mesa, a modern complex with a hotel, restaurant, and shops. Others work at the trading post, for the reservation health service, or as teachers or police officers.

Another tribal business is the Hopi Three Canyon Ranches. As well as grazing cattle on this land, the Hopis have extended the business to encourage the hunting of elk and antelopes.

Many Hopis make crafts to sell to tourists. Men carve kachina dolls, craft silver, or weave cotton. Women of each

This Second Mesa woman uses traditional techniques and designs to make coiled baskets and trays for tourists.

mesa specialize in a craft: the First Mesa women make pottery, Second Mesa women weave trays with yucca, and Third Mesa women form trays from colorful wicker.

HOPI ARTS

CHAPTER 11

The Hopis have always had a rich and varied artistic tradition, which continues to this day. Kachina doll carving has remained a strong artistic tradition among the Hopis, and many men carve these representatives of the Hopi spirit world.

One of the most famous Native American potters is Nampeyo, a Hopi-Tewa. Born in 1860, she began making clay pots at a time when the Hopis were starting to use American factory-made pottery. Nampeyo's use of ancient Hopi designs turned the useful pots into beautiful art. Her pots are the only ones from that time recognized and collected as art.

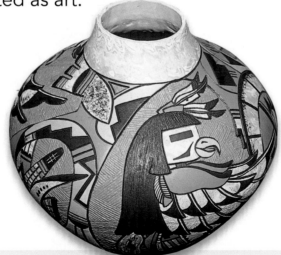

Made from the clay found near the First Mesa, Hopi pottery features three colors patterned in traditional designs.

Nampeyo was a potter-in-residence at the Grand Canyon's Hopi House and inspired many potters who came after her, including her daughters, grandchildren, and great-grandchildren. Her great-granddaughter Dextra Quotskuyva is probably the best known of them. She studied and gained inspiration from Hopi pottery designs from the 16th and 17th centuries. In all her work she used traditional materials, such as dried gourds for scraping and strips of yucca for painting. Where possible, her paints were made from local plants and rocks. Despite the influence of traditional materials and designs, Quotskuyva is celebrated for creating many new decorative ideas.

kachina doll

THE HOPI ECONOMY

CHAPTER 12

Though many Native American tribes have raised money for their people by owning **casinos**, the Hopis have not, believing that gambling is not the Hopi way. This has led to fewer jobs on the reservation, and young people often leave to find work elsewhere.

Coal mining is a **controversial** issue among the Hopis. The Hopi operating **budget** depends upon income from Peabody Energy, which mines coal at the Kayenta Mine on Black Mesa. The Black Mesa Mine was closed in 2005 because of its impact on the **environment**. Many Hopis want the Black Mesa Mine reopened. Others, organized as the Black Mesa Trust, want all coal mining to stop. They have gone to court and campaigned for solar energy instead. The tribal council, which supports more mining, has tried to ban **environmentalists** from entering the reservation.

One other source of income—tourism—also remains controversial. Tourists are a good source of income, but they are very disruptive to the Hopi lifestyle;

The Black Mesa Mine provided jobs for the Hopis between 1970 and 2005, but it also destroyed sacred sites, caused pollution, and reduced water supplies.

many Hopis don't like to have tourists attending their ceremonies and festivities. In fact, some villages have posted signs that say that white outsiders are not allowed in the village or are not allowed to attend Hopi ceremonies.

HOPI ISSUES TODAY
CHAPTER 13

As with many other Native American nations, the independent Hopi Nation faces the issue of continuing their traditional culture. Because they remain isolated on the remote Arizona mesas, they have been more successful than most tribes.

However, the Hopi people face a continuing water crisis. There are no rivers or lakes on Hopi lands; Hopis depend upon rain for farming and wells for their water. Drinking water comes from the Navajo Aquifer, an underground body of water beneath Black Mesa. This water was used to move the coal from the Black Mesa Mine through a pipeline 273 miles (440 km) long for use at a **power plant** in Laughlin, Nevada. Peabody Coal was using 120,000 gallons (462,000 l) of water an hour, and the Hopis feared that they were running out of water.

In 2005, the highly polluting power plant at Laughlin closed. Mining at Black Mesa Mine was halted also. The nearby Kayenta Mine is still working, but does not use the Navajo Aquifer.

Soon, the traditional Hopi farming method of using only rainwater to irrigate crops may not supply enough food for all the people. Farmers are looking for other water sources.

Severe drought in 2014 rekindled the land dispute between Hopis and the Navajo. Navajo grazing animals were impounded after being caught on Hopi land. The Hopis argued that they were trying to conserve their remaining resources.

GLOSSARY

adobe: Built out of bricks made of clay or earth and dried in the sun.

adolescent: Having to do with the process of changing from a child to an adult.

boarding school: A school that both teaches and houses children.

budget: The amount of money available for a period of time and the planned or expected expenses.

casino: A place where gambling takes place.

clan: A group of related families.

conscientious objector: Someone who refuses to become a soldier because of their religious or moral beliefs.

controversial: Causing widespread disagreement.

culture: The arts, beliefs, and customs that form a people's way of life.

environment: The natural world.

environmentalist: Someone who wants to protect the natural world.

initiated: Given permission to enter a certain group and share secret information.

kiva: A special underground room used only for religious and ceremonial purposes by men.

mesa: A wide, flat mountaintop with cliffs on all sides.

mission: A church or group of buildings where people of one religion try to teach people of another religion their beliefs.

negotiation: A discussion to reach an agreement on a problem.

power plant: A place where electricity is created.

private property: Land or objects that belong only to one person.

pueblo: A Native American village in the Southwest.

Pueblo Indians: Native American tribes who live in the deserts of the American Southwest.

reservation: Land set aside by the government for specific Native American tribes to live on.

revolt: A rebellion or uprising against rulers.

ritual: Formal ceremonies.

solstice: One of two days during the year when the sun reaches the farthest north and the farthest south.

sue: To take legal action against a person or an institution.

trespass: Enter someone else's property without permission.

FOR MORE INFORMATION

BOOKS

Dwyer, Helen. *Peoples of the Southwest, West, and North.* Redding, CT: Brown Bear Books, 2009.

Manning, Jack. *Pueblos.* North Mankato, MN: Capstone Press, 2015.

Pritzker, Barry. *The Hopi.* New York, NY: Chelsea House, 2011.

WEBSITES

Due to the changing nature of Internet links, PowerKids Press has developed an online list of websites related to the subject of this book. This site is updated regularly. Please use this link to access the list: www.powerkidslinks.com/sona/hopi

INDEX

A

Arizona, 4, 5, 6, 17, 28

B

Black Mesa, 5, 26, 27, 28

C

Calhoun, John, 8, 9
ceremonies, 17, 18, 20, 21, 22, 27
children, 18, 22
clans, 14, 16, 17, 21
coal mining, 26, 27

F

First Mesa, 4, 23, 24
Friendlies, 10, 11

H

Hopi Tribal Council, 11, 12, 26
Hostiles, 10, 11

I

Indian Reorganization Act, 11

K

kachina, 16, 22
kachina dolls, 22, 24, 25
Keams Canyon, 8
kikmongwi, 12, 17
kivas, 6, 18, 20

M

Mexico, 7, 8, 14
missions, 6, 8

N

Navajo, 4, 6, 9, 12, 13, 29
Navajo-Hopi Land Settlement Act,
12

O

Oraibi, 6, 10, 11

P

pottery, 23, 24, 25
Pueblo Indians, 4, 6, 10
Pueblo Revolt, 6

R

reservation, 4, 8, 9, 12, 22, 26

S

Second Mesa, 4, 22, 23
societies, 16, 17, 18, 19
Spanish, 6, 7, 14

T

Third Mesa, 4, 23
tourism, 26

U

United States, 8, 10, 12

V

village crier, 17, 21

W

World War II, 12, 13